MW01092618

THE POWER
OF PARTNERSHIP

Andrew Wommack

Published in partnership between Andrew Wommack Ministries and Harrison House Publishers.

Woodland Park, CO 80863 – Shippensburg, PA 17257

ISBN 13 TP: 978-1-59548-593-9

For Worldwide Distribution, Printed in the USA

1 2 3 4 5 6 / 26 25 24 23

Contents

Introduction

I know that when ministers go to talking about money, most people head for the exits. They don't like to hear about those things from preachers, and there is a real resistance to it. But giving of your finances not only blesses the ministry or church you're giving to, but it's also beneficial to you. I don't think most people really understand this. If they did, they would be involved in partnership because it is a powerful thing.

Are you believing for prosperity, but still struggling financially? Are you giving, but not seeing a harvest on the seeds you're sowing? There is a way for you to prosper financially and grow spiritually, and I believe it begins with partnership.

There is truth to prosperity, and specifically what I'm going to be teaching in this booklet is how partnership benefits you. If you throw the baby out with

1

the bath water because some people have manipulated and used the Scripture incorrectly for selfish motivation, you're going to miss out on a blessing.

It seems like people will go and hear somebody talk about how they make money in the stock market, and they'll get excited about that. They'll go and listen to somebody talk about how they made money buying houses, fixing them up, and then flipping them. As long as it's outside of spiritual things, people are seeking ways to prosper. But when a preacher starts talking about money, I guarantee there will be resistance. Now, I understand some of it is well-deserved. Many ministers speak about finances because it's a way of guilting and manipulating people, causing them to give. But that's a Judas attitude.

In John 12:3–5, when a woman was anointing Jesus with expensive perfumed oil, the disciple who would betray Him complained, *"Why was not this ointment sold for three hundred pence ("a year's wages"* according to *the New Living Translation), and given to the poor?"* There are a lot of people, even in the church, who say something similar when a Christian begins to really prosper. I'll tell you, if you have that kind of Judas spirit on you, that's not a good thing!

I've actually had people get mad at me for teaching on finances, prosperity, and partnership. Back when I was ministering on radio, before I started on television, I had a man write and threaten to sue me for using radio time to teach people about money. He said that I should have been using that airtime to deal with just the basics of Christianity and telling people about getting saved.

Jesus says just the opposite. He said if you aren't faithful in that which is least, then you won't be faithful in greater things (Luke 16:9–10). In other words, if you can't trust God in this area of finances, then you won't be able to trust Him in other areas.

If you are willing to take a portion of what's yours and commit to giving it on a regular basis to a church or ministry, that's partnership. And I believe it will begin a supernatural flow in your life!

Partnership Benefits You

Years ago, one of our Charis Bible College graduates invited me to minister at a church up in the mountains of Colorado. He pastored a small church with about twenty or thirty people. It was such a small group that he invited two other churches to join the meeting, so altogether there were around a hundred people who attended.

Because it was a small number of people, they were afraid that they wouldn't get very much money in the offerings. So, they offered to let me take up my own offering. I can only assume they were thinking if I was the one that received the offerings, then I couldn't complain about the results. But it didn't matter to me. I usually let whoever is hosting the meeting receive the offerings. I never go anywhere because of money.

Before going to this little church in the mountains, I had just come from ministering in Charlotte, North Carolina; and each time I held a meeting there, the church gave me anywhere from $50,000 to $300,000 for a week of services. That church gave me the largest gifts of any that I'd ever been to up to that time.

So, I started this meeting by saying, "I just came from a church that gave me a huge offering. I am not a poor pastor that just barely got into town and who, if you don't give won't be able to get out of town. I'm not here because I need things. I don't need your money." When I did that, you could just see all of the blood drain out of the face of this pastor on the front row.

The way most people receive an offering is all about satisfying a need—and I understand that. The Bible says in 1 John 3:17 that if you see your brother or a sister in need and *"shutteth up [your] bowels of* compassion *from [them], how dwelleth the love of God in [you]?"* So, giving to a person in need is a valid reason. It's probably the simplest motive for giving, but that's not all that there is to it. Giving is also good for you!

When I teach on finances, I don't do it to benefit me. It's for you! It's just like when I teach on healing, I don't teach it for my sake. Now, it does benefit me because I believe the Word, and as I speak it out of my mouth, I get blessed by it and believe that it helps me (Rom. 10:17). But the primary reason I teach on healing isn't so that I can be healed; it's to share the truth with you so that you can be healed.

The reason I teach on emotions, walking in joy, how to believe God, and all these other things isn't for me. I do it for you. But when I start teaching about money, people immediately think that it is totally selfish—that the reason I teach on finances is because I need finances.

> **When I teach on finances, I don't do it to benefit me. It's for you!**

Now, it's true that we need money to get things done, and God will bless me. But I want to share the benefit that giving has toward you.

Giving Is Like a Seed

I approached the offering at that meeting hosted by those three little churches as a blessing to those who give. I said, "It's not about what my need is. You need to give. You need to be a part of what God is doing.

You need to take a portion of what God has given you, and you need to use it for something besides yourself."

I used the example of giving being like a seed. In 2 Corinthians 9:10, the apostle Paul talks about how God gives seed to the sower. I told them that if you eat all of your seed and don't plant some of it, then you're going to be hungry. You have to recognize the potential that is in that seed for your future, and you have to discipline yourself and plant some of it or you're going to be hungry tomorrow. So, I taught on all these things, and it was really good!

The next week, after that meeting was over, the pastor of that little church called me and explained that when I started saying, "I don't need your money," he thought it would kill the offering. But as it turned out, they wound up giving the largest offering to me that they had ever given to anybody.

He told me that on the following Sunday morning, he got up in front of his church—the twenty to thirty people that regularly attended—and said, "I don't remember the messages that Andrew taught on. All I remember are those offering talks." He went on to say, "I knew these things, but I hadn't shared them with you because there is a resistance to ministers teaching about money."

Personally, that pastor operated in giving, but he didn't challenge his church to give because he was afraid the people would think he was doing it for the wrong reasons. He fell on his knees, began to cry, and asked his church to forgive him. He asked them to forgive him for not telling the truth and taking away opportunities to prosper because he was afraid of what people would think.

He just repented right there in front of his whole church. And the people came up, started hugging him, and saying, "Pastor, we forgive you." After that, people started giving. They gave tens of thousands of dollars just on that Sunday morning, paid off the entire church debt, caused prosperity to come, and sparked a revival in that ministry. I'll tell you, this is the power of partnership!

There's a difference between just giving every once in a while and giving regularly. Maybe you are giving emotionally when there is a problem or a need, so you just scatter your seed and throw it. You'll get some response from that, but you should start partnering with ministries and give deliberately, spacing it out, setting aside on the first day every single week (as Paul said in 1 Cor. 16:1–2) what you are going to give to God. When you start giving deliberately like that, it's like planting in furrows and spacing your seeds versus just throwing your seeds here and there. I believe you will receive a much greater return! Partnership is of course beneficial to the church or to the ministry that you give to, but partnership is also beneficial to you, and I don't think most people really understand that.

Parable of the Unjust Steward

In Luke 16:1–8, Jesus taught the parable of the unjust steward. It's a story about a man who was a steward of another man's business. This steward had been accused of stealing money from his master (v. 1), so the master confronted him and demanded to see the books (v. 2). Essentially, the master here is saying, "If what I've heard is true, then you're going to be out of a job." So, the steward panicked because he had been stealing and knew that he was going to be fired.

The steward then called all of his master's debtors together, and he discounted their debts (vv. 5–7)— some 50 percent and some 20 percent. It was like the steward was saying to the debtors, "You owe $100,000, but if you'll give me $50,000 right now, we'll settle your bill." He discounted their debts so that when he was kicked out of his master's house, he'd be able to go knock on the doors of all of these people and say, "Do you remember what I did for you? Now, could you do something for me?" He was working on the presumption these people would feel obligated to give him food, let him stay in their homes, or help him in some way.

So, he was still stealing money from his master by discounting the money that was owed without permission. But instead of sticking the money in his pocket, he was putting it in other people's pockets. In a sense, it was a bribe so he could have some help when he lost his job.

There's something strange that happened, though. In verse 8, Jesus says,

And the lord commended the unjust steward, because he had done wisely: for the children of this world are in their generation wiser than the children of light.

Now why would he commend this guy? Well, I think the reason is because he finally began to realize the power of money to affect the future.

Then, in verse 9, Jesus gave His disciples the practical application of the parable by saying,

Make to yourselves friends of the mammon of unrighteousness; that, when ye fail, they may receive you into everlasting habitations.

Now this is the *King James Version* that I'm quoting here, but it's not that hard to understand. He's just saying that you should use money to touch people's lives. Jesus is trying to get His disciples to recognize the power that's in money to touch people's lives so that when we die and enter into heaven, there will be people lined up to welcome us. Because we give to a ministry or missions work, there will be people in heaven we would have never been able to otherwise reach because we used the power of money for the Gospel.

Whether you like it or not, money does give you influence. It gives you power. It gives you the ability to do things that you couldn't do if you didn't have money. So, there is power in money, but the sad thing is most people are using that power, that influence, shortsightedly. They are blowing it on material things and aren't thinking long term.

Money gives you power, and there is some security in money, but we shouldn't put our faith in it. We ought to put our faith in the one who has prospered us and has given us the power to get wealth—God (Deut. 8:18).

Opening a Supernatural Flow

I remember when I was in Hong Kong speaking at a ministers' conference. I really felt like God told me to minister on finances and a right attitude toward prosperity. Since it was a ministers' conference, I felt like the Lord specifically wanted me to minister against the fear that ministers have about receiving offerings. But to be honest with you, I had a fear about ministering that myself.

As I've traveled the United States, I've found that when a minister mentions money, it immediately turns people off. There's rejection. Some people even get up and leave. And outside of the United States, it's a hundred times worse. Part of this is because American pastors have

> We ought to put our faith in the one who has prospered us and has given us the power to get wealth.

gone all over the world raising money and have a very bad reputation because of it. So, I just knew that there was going to be pushback when I ministered on finances in Hong Kong.

I knew that it wasn't going to be popular if I mentioned money. So, I didn't do it. I ministered on something else and really disobeyed God. It wasn't intentional, but I just thought, *God, this won't go over well.* Later, when I went out to lunch with the pastor and his staff after the morning message, he told me how his church was struggling financially. "We need help with finances," he said. "Would you please share?" So, all during lunch, I taught for hours to his staff. When that happened, it was like the Lord just confirmed what I was supposed to minister on.

In the afternoon, when I got up to minister at the conference, I said, "I'm going to change the whole focus of everything I'm doing. I'm going to minister on something that you may not like." I asked the audience, "If you could name one thing that you do not want to hear an American preacher teach on, what would it be?" And immediately, out of the crowd of about 300 people, they started saying, "money," "finances," and "prosperity." So, I responded, "Well, that's exactly what God told me to minister on."

I started ministering on it and, I'll tell you, it was some hard ground at first. It was rough plowing, but by the end of that conference, we had so many people have breakthroughs in the area of finances.

I have seen hundreds of thousands of people who have received revelation about money and trusting God—putting Him first ahead of their money. When people do that, it just starts a supernatural flow in their lives, and not only a flow of money. Yes, if you *"give . . . it shall be given unto you; good measure, pressed down, and shaken together, and running over"* (Luke 6:38a), but it also starts a continual flow of God's blessings toward you when you start trusting God in this area of money. It's a reflection of a person's maturity when they begin to give faithfully and joyfully.

Jesus was saying that if you aren't faithful in that which is least—money—then how can you be trusted with greater riches (Luke 16:10–13). If you can't believe God and use your faith and give and trust that when you give it's going to be given back to you, then you're just fooling yourself to think that you can trust God for your healing, deliverance, marriage, salvation, or other things. Jesus says trusting God in this area of money is the least use of your faith.

> **It's a reflection of a person's maturity when they begin to give faithfully and joyfully.**

Let me put it this way. As I've traveled and ministered for over fifty years, I have met thousands of people. And I cannot name one person who I consider to be a mature, stable Christian who doesn't trust God in the area of finances.

Fellowship in the Gospel

In Philippians 1:3, Paul wrote, "*I thank my God upon every remembrance of you.*" I don't believe Paul did this for every single person. He was writing to a special group of people in Philippi, and I think it was because of their partnership—because of the way these people received him and enabled him to go and reach other people.

> *I thank my God upon every remembrance of you, Always in every prayer of mine for you all making request with joy, For your fellowship in the gospel from the first day until now.*
>
> Philippians 1:3–5

This word *"fellowship"* in these verses is translated from the Greek word *koinonia*, which also means partnership.[1] He is thanking God for their partnership in the Gospel. As a matter of fact, this was the only church that supported him after he left that area. Now, it's one thing when a minister comes to your church and you give because you receive something, or you go and buy a product. In a sense, that's paying for what you're getting. But when you start giving beyond what it costs for you to receive, and you start giving so the minister can go and share the Gospel with somebody else, that's partnership. This is what Paul is talking about.

These people in Philippi were partners with him, and in Philippians 4:17, Paul said he was not saying these things *"because I desire a gift: but I desire fruit that may abound to your account."* He was praising God that these people had given, not just because it had helped him, but because it was going to come back unto them a hundredfold in this life (Mark 10:30). Paul was rejoicing because these people were his partners. They had given to him even after he left. And Paul said Philippi was the only church that ever did this.

In the body of Christ today, we have fallen a long way from the New Testament church in a lot of respects. But I think this is something that we are doing better than the New Testament church did. I think we give more financially and support ministers and missions better than the early church.

We don't know exactly how long Paul ministered, but it may have been thirty years or more. And during this period of time, he traveled extensively. He did it at great expense to himself. He even had to make tents in many places, working a secular job to support himself and the people that traveled with him (2 Cor. 11:25–28). And yet, out of all of these people that he ministered to, the Philippians were the only people who ever sent money to help him after he left the local area. I think that's tragic.

Today, we do better than that. Our ministry has tens of thousands of partners that help me to send the Gospel all over the world. In the same way, this is the reason Paul rejoiced every time he thought of the Philippians for their fellowship or partnership in the Gospel.

Promises of Partnership

The book of Philippians was written to Paul's partners. I think it's important for us to recognize that, because some of these scriptures we use all of the time and apply to every single person really do not apply. Paul was writing specifically to partners.

In Philippians 1:6, Paul wrote,

Being confident of this very thing, that he which hath begun a good work in you will perform it *until the day of Jesus Christ.*

I hear people use this all of the time and say, "I am confident that God is going to continue the good work that He began in me." Now, I know that God wants to continue the good work. God is not willing for a single person to lose the things that He has spoken to you and done in your life. But I am not confident that every person reading this booklet is going to have God perform it. That's not because God doesn't want to do it, but because we have to cooperate.

God's will doesn't just automatically come to pass in your life. Jesus said in Matthew 7:7,

> *Ask, and it shall be given you; seek, and ye shall find; knock, and it shall be opened unto you.*

You've got to participate. You've got to seek the Lord.

Through the prophet, God says in Jeremiah 29:11,

> *I know the thoughts that I think toward you, saith the Lord, thoughts of peace, and not of evil, to give you an expected end.*

The *NIV* renders the end of that verse as *"a hope and a future."* Now, this is a passage of Scripture that's become very popular, and you'll hear it quoted a lot. And I do believe that God has good plans for every single person. But not every person is going to experience those good plans. In verses 12 and 13 of that same chapter, the Lord goes on to say, *"Then . . . ye shall seek me, and find me, when ye shall search for me with all your heart."* People have to seek God to receive His expected end for them.

Likewise, in Philippians 1:6, God has good plans, and He wants to continue and complete the work that he's begun in you. But it's not going to happen without your cooperation. Paul was able to say this to the Philippians because these people had moved beyond being takers—people that were using the Gospel and the freedom that God gave

> God's will doesn't just automatically come to pass in your life.

them just to set themselves free. The Philippians had been set free by God, but then they wanted to see other people set free and became partners with the apostle Paul. They sent money and helped him when he went to minister to people in another place (Phil. 4:15–16).

Also, when Paul was in Rome, the Bible said he dwelt two whole years in prison (Acts 28:30–31), but it wasn't in a Roman prison. He lived in a hired house that gave him some freedom and allowed him to write a good portion of the New Testament. He also shared the Gospel with the emperor, and the Scripture says there were many in Caesar's household who believed (Phil. 4:22).

Now, how does a prisoner pay for a house? It was people that Paul had ministered to who enabled him to pay for his own house arrest for two years. He wasn't able to work or make any money for himself. It came from partners!

Seek First the Kingdom

Paul was saying that partnership will yield fruit that will abound to your account (Phil. 4:17). If you would open up your heart and let the Holy Spirit give you a revelation about this, it would change your whole paradigm. Instead of thinking about how much you can get, you can start thinking of how you can give to others, and you will just receive through a supernatural flow.

Basically, the American dream is, get all you can, can all you get, and then sit on your can. That's the way most people approach life. But I hope you can understand that you can take money and turn something that is paper, coins, or precious metals—something that someday is going to be destroyed—and turn it into something eternal.

Someday, money will be gone. This whole earth is going to be destroyed with a *"fervent heat"* (2 Pet. 3:10–12), and I can guarantee if you build your life on material things, it's all going to be gone someday. It doesn't matter how you try and invest your money. Even if you put it into diamonds, the hardest substance we know, someday it is going to be melted and go away. But if you take a portion of what you have and invest it in changing people's lives, then something that is temporary and has an expiration date—money—can be turned into something—changed lives—that will benefit you throughout eternity. Instead of praying, "God, how much can I get?" or "How big can my house be?" you'd be asking how you could bless someone.

How big does your house have to be? How many beds do you sleep in at night? I mean, how big does your bathroom have to be for you to take care of business? I've traveled a lot and been in homes all over the world, and the typical American bathroom is bigger than most people's bedrooms. I'm not saying that God doesn't want you to have a nice place. God is El Shaddai, not "El Cheapo"! But I am saying that most people's focus is on finances for themselves.

Paul is essentially saying, "I don't desire your partnership because it benefits me. I desire fruit that may abound to your account." That fruit includes finances so you can prosper here in this life, but it's primarily eternal. When you become a partner, it yields returns that are out of this world. A person would be foolish to take something like money that is going to perish, and not turn it into something that is eternal. If we were long-term thinkers—if we were thinking about eternity—I guarantee you, we would handle our finances much differently.

Matthew 6:33 says if you could get to where you *"seek . . . first the kingdom of God, and his righteousness"*—not secondly, not thirdly, not after all of your needs are taken care of—then *"all these things shall be added unto you."* The things that are listed in those verses around it include what you eat, where you sleep, and what you're clothed with (Matt. 6:25–34). In other words, God would take care of your needs supernaturally if you would just put Him first.

Give and It Will Be Given

I'll tell you, if God can get his money through you to establish the kingdom and to bless other people, then He'll get it to you. The Bible says over in 2 Corinthians 9:10,

Now he that ministereth seed to the sower both minister bread for your food, and multiply your seed sown, and increase the fruits of your righteousness.

This says that God gives seed to sowers, but this isn't talking about physical seed. It's using that as an example of money. Every verse in the eighth and ninth chapters of 2 Corinthians is talking about money. Money is compared to seed because you can consume it yourself, and it will help you. But if you consume all of it and don't sow some, you're going to eventually be hungry because there won't be a new harvest to eat from.

> **When you become a partner, it yields returns that are out of this world.**

You can spend money on yourself, and it's good to meet your obligations, but you need to be smart enough to sow some of it, or you're going to wind up being without in the future. If you find you are constantly short of money, it may be that God doesn't see you as a giver. He sees you as a taker. He gives seed to sowers or givers.

Some people are like a vacuum cleaner that's just going around and constantly sucking everything toward themselves. It's like they are saying, "My name is Jimmy! Gimmie, gimmie, gimmie!" That's the attitude of most people who consume everything. But if God can find somebody who is a giver—a sower, God will give seed to that person. If He can get it through you, He will get it to you. That's powerful!

Some of you reading this may be thinking, *This doesn't make sense. I don't have enough money for everything I want right now, and if I start taking a portion of what I got and I give it away, I'm going to have even less. I'm not moving toward my goals. I'm moving away from them!*

That would be true if there wasn't a God who also promised when you give, *"it shall be given unto you; good measure, pressed down, and shaken together, and running over, shall men give into your bosom"* (Luke 6:38). If there wasn't a God who promised that He would give seed to people who give, then it would be true that to take a portion of what you have and give it away would put you farther away from your goals. But we have a God who will prosper you and promised that when you put *"first the kingdom of God, and his righteousness"* (Matt. 6:33), He will give you all these other things.

The way to prosperity isn't by hoarding and holding on to things; it's by opening up your hands and sowing and giving. You can give your way into prosperity.

To date, we have given away hundreds of millions of copies of more than 400 of my teachings via books, CDs, DVDs, and downloads from our website. In the natural, that just doesn't make any sense. And yet God has just blessed us because of it.

I know some of you are thinking, *I just don't believe that.* Well then, it won't work for you! But if you will believe these truths I'm sharing and mix them with faith (Heb. 4:2), you will see that this is how to prosper. You need to become a giver. You need to become a partner!

Giving Motivated by Love

Even though giving is good, it does take more than just plunking something in a bucket. Your heart has to have the right motivation, and that's why being a partner is so powerful. Partnership requires more than just giving money.

If all there was to prosperity is just a *"give, and it shall be given unto you"* hundredfold return (Mark 10:30), then every person who's given $1,000 would've already received back $1 million. But that hasn't happened. I can guarantee there are people who have given, it hasn't come back to them, and they haven't seen those results. Is it because the Word isn't true? No! It's because there's more to prosperity than just giving and having it automatically happen.

> You can give your way into prosperity.

The thirteenth chapter of 1 Corinthians is what's commonly called "the love chapter." For example, in verse 3, Paul said,

And though I bestow all my goods to feed the poor, *and though I give my body to be burned, and have not charity, it profiteth me nothing.*

The word *charity* used here in the *King James Version* means God's kind of love. It's saying if you give everything you have to feed the poor, or if you made the ultimate sacrifice and gave your body to be burned, and if you didn't do it motivated by love, it profits you nothing. That is a huge statement!

Paul is saying that the motive behind your giving is more important than your giving. This is the reason some of you have given, and yet you haven't seen it returned to you. Maybe you gave, but you weren't doing it with the right heart and attitude. Many people give because they are begged, pressured, or condemned.

You may have given for all these other reasons, but you weren't giving out of God's kind of love, and the Scripture says in Galatians 5:6 that faith works by love. You have to give in faith motivated by love. You have to give with some understanding and belief about what you're doing, but so many people just give emotionally.

I was at a woman's house one time, and she showed me a letter. It was sent from a minister who supposedly put her name in there and said, "God woke me up at three o'clock this morning and told me that you were believing for someone to be saved, someone that you love. And if you will send a $1,000 offering today, God has told me your loved one will be saved!" This lady's name was interspersed throughout the entire thing, as if that minister was writing directly to her.

Here was this woman, crying and saying to me, "I've been praying and believing for someone to be saved, and I know that this must be God because He woke him up at three in the morning and told him this. But I don't have $1,000! What do I do?" I could tell she was heartbroken, so I just took that letter, tore it into pieces, and threw it in the trash. I said, "That's what you do!"

I told her, "This man didn't wake up at three o'clock in the morning and get your name from God. This is a computer-generated letter!" I've been around a lot of ministers, and I've seen a lot of things. I realized that if she gave to this minister, she would give out of debt or obligation. It would profit her nothing. The motive behind your gift is more important than your gift!

Gifts Make Room for You

A man's gift maketh room for him, and bringeth him before great men.

Proverbs 18:16

For years, I thought this was talking about how a person's anointing, talent, or ability will promote them, open a door, and bring them before great men. But as I studied this more, I found that's not what it's talking about. The Hebrew word translated *"gift"* here in Proverbs 18:16, means a present.[2] It's talking about a gift—a physical or a monetary gift—that makes room for you and brings you before great men. Now, there's a lot of people who don't like this. They take offense and say, "This is like a bribe. You're using money to manipulate people."

Money is not moral or immoral; it's amoral. You can use money to get a person to do something they don't want to do, but you could also use that same money to bless a person. You can take $100 and use it to pay a prostitute or bribe a politician, or you could give it to someone and say, "God loves you." It's really not the money that is right or wrong. It's the motivation of the heart.

You can use money to open up a door for you spiritually. You can tap into the anointing that is on a person. When you start giving, it opens up a door to you in the spiritual realm. It releases something into your life. That's probably a brand-new thought for a lot of people, but I believe that's exactly what Proverbs 18:16 is saying—money opens up a door for you and brings you before great men.

The same Hebrew word that was translated "gift" in Proverbs 18:16 was also translated "gift" in Proverbs 19:6b.[3] That verse says,

Every man is *a friend to him that giveth gifts.*

Obviously, this verse isn't speaking about some talent or ability. It is speaking of a financial or material gift. That's also the way it is being used in Proverbs 18:16.

When the Queen of Sheba came to King Solomon seeking wisdom (1 Kgs. 10:1–13), she brought with her a train of gifts, including gold, precious stones, and spices. As a matter of fact, the value of the gold alone—120 talents (v. 10), which converts to about 145,000 ounces[4]—would be hundreds of millions of dollars in today's market.[5] Those gifts gave her access to the king's presence, and *"she communed with him of all that was in her heart"* (v. 2). In return, Solomon *"told her all her questions: there was not any thing hid from the king, which he told her not"* (v. 3). He *"gave unto the queen of Sheba all her desire, whatsoever she asked"* (v. 13).

Now, if I wanted to speak with the president of the United States or some other national leader, I couldn't just walk in off the street and do that. But the Queen of Sheba used a financial gift to give her access. The same is true in the spiritual realm.

Charlie and Jill LeBlanc have been part of the worship at our events for years. As they traveled many years ago, they used to give to small churches who were struggling. They gave where they thought it would do the most good. But then Charlie and Jill got the revelation that they needed to sow where they wanted to go and not just to help people in need. They had a desire to reach more people with their music. After understanding that their giving could make room for them, they began giving to a ministry that had grown to have a worldwide influence. It wasn't long before this ministry invited Charlie and Jill to lead worship at their meetings. They suddenly went from ministering in small venues to traveling the world for several years and seeing tens of thousands of people come to those meetings.

Charlie and Jill just started having this huge exposure, and it came because this minister said, "I thought about you doing praise and worship for us, but the first thing I did was go check your giving to see if you were partners with us." Their consistent giving through partnership made room for them and led to promotion!

Drawing upon the Anointing

When you partner with a ministry, you not only bless the people who are being touched by that ministry, but you also start a supernatural flow of your finances, and you partake of the anointing and the blessing that's on that minister's life. It's not bad to want the anointing that is on my life or that of another minister.

When I was first getting started on television years ago, we were covering about 3 percent of the homes in the United States, and the Lord told me I was limiting Him by my small thinking. So, I began to believe for increase. I was friends with a minister who was further down the road than I was in television ministry, and they were believing God to go on a large network. They were believing for a lot of money to purchase the necessary equipment to get this done. I was at a meeting where they were sharing this vision, so I committed to sow $3,000 a month, which at that time was a lot of money for me. But I knew I needed increase in my own television ministry.

I sowed into this ministry on a monthly basis, specifically so that my gift would make room for me and bring me before great men (Prov. 18:16). I believed my gift would tap into the anointing on this ministry, which was already reaching more people than we were. I sowed into their project to bless them, and those gifts became part of their supply; but also I saw that it was a way of drawing that anointing that was on them toward me.

It's like if you're thirsty for water and you see a river flowing by, you could dip your hand in there and get enough water to help you in that moment; or you could dig a channel and divert some of that water toward you as a continual flow. If you kept digging, you could actually change the entire course of that river. When you give and become a partner with people, in a sense, that's what you're doing.

You may see a powerful anointing on a person or on a ministry and say, "I want some of that." Instead of just getting enough for a moment by giving once or buying a product, you can actually become a partner with them. When you do that, your gifts open doors. Your giving makes room for you, brings you before great men, and will start drawing their anointing toward you.

Here we are, years after I sowed into that ministry's project, and our television program can now be seen by billions of people. As of this writing, it can be watched practically everywhere in the English-speaking world, over eleven time zones in Russia, the Middle East, and around the globe. My program is also translated into eight foreign languages. And we're seeing awesome things happen.

Praise God, the Gospel's going deeper and farther than ever before! We've seen a huge increase in our television ministry, and I believe it's because when I was believing to increase our reach, my gifts made room and brought us before great men. It's important to understand the power that is available in partnership and then put that power to work for you!

Not Room Enough to Receive

In the fifth chapter of Luke, Jesus came and ministered to the multitudes with the help of Simon (who later became Peter). The people were thronging Jesus (v. 1), so He entered into a fishing boat with Simon (v. 3). Jesus needed to have some separation between Himself and the people so He could minister to everyone effectively. You've got to remember, at that time, they didn't have public address systems like we have now.

One of the ways that a person can amplify their voice is by speaking across the surface of a body of water. So, He asked Simon, "Can I get into your boat and go out a little bit from the shore?" By agreeing to go out on the water, Simon gave use of his boat to Jesus and became a partner with Him.

Simon was helping Jesus reach all of this multitude who wanted to hear the Word, so he partnered with Jesus, and look what happened. After Jesus got through ministering to the people, He said in verse 4,

Simon, Launch out into the deep, and let down your nets for a draught.

Simon had given to Jesus and enabled Him to do something. Because of it, Jesus was going to bless him back—and Jesus wanted to bless him more than what Simon was able to receive. In other words, if you give, Jesus is not going to ever let you out give Him. When you give, it'll be given back unto you, pressed down, shaken together, and running over (Luke 6:38).

Jesus told Simon to let down the "nets" (plural), and yet Simon only let down a "net" (singular). Simon wasn't expecting much because he said, *"Master, we have toiled all the night, and have taken nothing"* (v. 5). The best time for fishing was at night, but here it was during the day. Simon and the other fisherman were getting ready to wash their nets for the next night. If they let them all down into the water, they'd have to wash them again. It was a bother to him, but he said, *"Nevertheless at thy word I will let down the net"* (v. 5).

Simon didn't know that God had already given a command to every fish in the Sea of Galilee to head for his boat, and that every one of them would try to cram into a single net. God wanted to bless Simon, and He did! Once Simon's net was filled to breaking (v. 6), he called for his partners, James and John. They brought their boat and nets, and they filled both the boats with so many fish, they began to sink (v. 7)! They didn't even have room enough to receive it!

This should remind you of what the Lord said in Malachi 3:10:

> *Bring ye all the tithes into the storehouse, that there may be meat in mine house, and prove me now herewith, saith the* LORD *of hosts, if I will not open you the windows of heaven, and pour you out a blessing, that* there shall *not* be room *enough* to receive it.

That's exactly what happened here! Simon and his partners didn't even have room enough to receive a harvest of fish that blessed them, their business, and their families.

God blessed them because of their partnership with Jesus, and this is exactly what happens when you partner with a church or ministry that's preaching the Gospel. That's the point I'm trying to make. It's obvious that when you give to a church or ministry that you bless them, but it's not as obvious that this is the way that God is going to bless you back. If you want to prosper, you need to start partnering with getting the Gospel out!

His Riches in Glory

I'm sharing all these truths in love (Eph. 4:15), and I'm not after you or your money. You don't necessarily have to give to me, though I believe this ministry is good soil. But you need to give to somebody! I know there are millions of people out there who are praying for God to prosper them. You may have even quoted Philippians 4:19, and said, "God, your Word says you'd supply all of my needs." But you first have to understand that Paul was writing to people who were partners.

People had gone beyond themselves, and they were giving a portion of their finances to share the Gospel with other people, and God supplied their needs. If you want to claim Philippians 4:19, you need to become a partner. You need to start giving beyond what it costs for you to receive, and quit tipping God.

You need to become a deliberate, purposeful, radical, fanatical, faith-filled giver, which is what I've been teaching in this booklet. And then, with authority, someone can say,

> *But my God shall supply all your need according to his riches in glory by Christ Jesus*
> Philippians 4:19

Notice Paul said it's according to God's riches in glory and not according to the economy or any man-made system. God will meet your needs supernaturally. In 2008–2009, when we had the so-called Great Recession, the stock market tanked. Whole fortunes collapsed, and people began to be fearful. People were even committing suicide.

In the Colorado Springs area, not far from where our ministry is located, there are literally hundreds of parachurch ministries. Many of them planned on having financial problems. They decreased their budgets. They began to start laying off people and preparing for disaster because that's what the world was saying. That's what was happening in the economy.

It was during that exact same time that God told me that I was supposed to start building a campus for our Charis Bible College. We actually bought a 157-acre piece of property in Woodland Park, Colorado, in 2009, and I started building in 2012. Since then, we have built more than $100 million worth of buildings debt-free.

When everybody else was cutting back, laying off people, and thinking small, I was increasing. It was the largest increase in our ministry up to that time. And I don't know of any ministry that has ever seen the same amount of increase over and above what it takes to maintain their television ministry and all the other things they might need. We spent more than $100 million in just over ten years on top of our normal expenses, and we are continuing to grow. The Lord has placed a vision on the inside of me for hundreds of millions of dollars' worth of new buildings on our campus, including student housing. It's going to be awesome! And the reason all that worked is because God supplied my need according to his riches in glory by Christ Jesus—not according to the economy.

There are people who honestly don't see God as their source. They see their job or something else as their source. But when you get into partnership, God will supply your need according to His riches in glory by Christ Jesus!

Conclusion

In this booklet, I've been teaching on partnership—that one of the ways you increase is to find a church, ministry, or someone who has the anointing of God upon them, and commit to give to them on a regular, consistent basis. When you find someone who is making a difference, and when you become a partner with them, the anointing, power, and prosperity on that ministry begins to flow toward you.

When you engage in partnership, there is a connection made, and a supernatural flow heads toward you. There's much more happening than just what's in the physical realm. There are spiritual dynamics at work. You and I can't see them, but in the Word of God, it says a man's gift makes room for him and brings him before great men (Prov. 18:16)—it taps into the power and anointing that's on a church or ministry.

I just encourage you to start being a partner—to go beyond what it takes for you to receive personally and start partnering with a church or a ministry that feeds you. Do it on a deliberate basis. Go beyond your need and start helping them to reach out and touch others.

Start giving on a deliberate, consistent, regular, and strategic basis. If you do that, I'm just telling you, there is going to be a supernatural flow towards you; and the sky is the limit! You're the only one who limits what God wants to do in your life, and I believe that this is going to help you take the limits off Him. You'll be blessed!

Further Study

If you enjoyed this booklet and would like to learn more about some of the things I've shared, I suggest my teachings:

- *The Power of Partnership* full-length teaching
- *Financial Stewardship*
- *Don't Limit God*
- *Excellence: How to Pursue an Excellent Spirit*
- *Financial Breakthroughs*

These teachings are available either free of charge at **awmi.net/video**, **awmi.net/audio**, or for purchase in book, study guide, CD, DVD, or USB formats at **awmi.net/store**.

Receive Jesus as Your Savior

Choosing to receive Jesus Christ as your Lord and Savior is the most important decision you'll ever make!

God's Word promises, *"That if thou shalt confess with thy mouth the Lord Jesus, and shalt believe in thine heart that God hath raised him from the dead, thou shalt be saved. For with the heart man believeth unto righteousness; and with the mouth confession is made unto salvation"* (Rom. 10:9–10). *"For whosoever shall call upon the name of the Lord shall be saved"* (Rom. 10:13). By His grace, God has already done everything to provide salvation. Your part is simply to believe and receive.

Pray out loud: "Jesus, I acknowledge that I've sinned and need to receive what you did for the for-giveness of my sins. I confess that You are my Lord and Savior. I believe in my heart that God raised You from the dead. By faith in Your Word, I receive salvation now. Thank You for saving me."

The very moment you commit your life to Jesus Christ, the truth of His Word instantly comes to pass in your spirit. Now that you're born again, there's a brand-new you!

Please contact us and let us know that you've prayed to receive Jesus as your Savior. We'd like to send you some free materials to help you on your new journey. Call our Helpline: **719-635-1111** (available 24 hours a day, seven days a week) to speak to a staff member who is here to help you understand and grow in your new relationship with the Lord.

Welcome to your new life!

Receive the Holy Spirit

As His child, your loving heavenly Father wants to give you the supernatural power you need to live a new life. *"For every one that asketh receiveth; and he that seeketh findeth; and to him that knocketh it shall be opened... how much more shall your heavenly Father give the Holy Spirit to them that ask him?"* (Luke 11:10–13).

All you have to do is ask, believe, and receive! Pray this: "Father, I recognize my need for Your power to live a new life. Please fill me with Your Holy Spirit. By faith, I receive it right now. Thank You for baptizing me. Holy Spirit, You are welcome in my life."

Some syllables from a language you don't recognize will rise up from your heart to your mouth (1 Cor. 14:14). As you speak them out loud by faith, you're releasing God's power from within and building yourself up in the spirit (1 Cor. 14:4). You can do this whenever and wherever you like.

It doesn't really matter whether you felt anything or not when you prayed to receive the Lord and His Spirit. If you believed in your heart that you received, then God's Word promises you did. *"Therefore I say unto you, What things soever ye desire, when ye pray, believe that ye receive* them, *and ye shall have* them" (Mark 11:24). God always honors His Word—believe it!

We would like to rejoice with you, pray with you, and answer any questions to help you understand more fully what has taken place in your life!

Please contact us to let us know that you've prayed to be filled with the Holy Spirit and to request the book *The New You & the Holy Spirit*. This book will explain in more detail about the benefits of being filled with the Holy Spirit and speaking in tongues. Call our Helpline: **719-635-1111** (available 24 hours a day, seven days a week).

Call for Prayer

If you need prayer for any reason, you can call our Helpline, 24 hours a day, seven days a week at **719-635-1111**. A trained prayer minister will answer your call and pray with you.

Every day, we receive testimonies of healings and other miracles from our Helpline, and we are ministering God's nearly-too-good-to-be-true message of the Gospel to more people than ever. So, I encourage you to call today!

About the Author

Andrew Wommack's life was forever changed the moment he encountered the supernatural love of God on March 23, 1968. As a renowned Bible teacher and author, Andrew has made it his mission to change the way the world sees God.

Andrew's vision is to go as far and deep with the Gospel as possible. His message goes far through the *Gospel Truth* television program, which is available to over half the world's population. The message goes deep through discipleship at Charis Bible College, headquartered in Woodland Park, Colorado. Founded in 1994, Charis has campuses across the United States and around the globe.

Andrew also has an extensive library of teaching materials in print, audio, and video. More than 200,000 hours of free teachings can be accessed at **awmi.net**.

Endnotes

1. Strong's Exhaustive Concordance of the Bible, "G2842, oinonia: fellowship," accessed March 1, 2023, https://biblehub.com/greek/2842.htm.

2. Brown-Driver-Briggs Lexicon, s.v. "וְתֵמ" ("matān"), accessed March 1, 2023, https://www.blueletterbible.org/lexicon/h4976/kjv/wlc/0-1/.

3. Strong's Exhaustive Concordance, s.v. "וְתֵמ" ("matān"), accessed March 1, 2023, https://www.blueletterbible.org/lexicon/h4976/kjv/wlc/0-1/.

4. "Convert Talent (Biblical Hebrew) to Pound," Unit Converters, accessed March 1, 2023, https://www.unitconverters.net/weight-and-mass/talent-biblical-hebrew-to-pound.htm.

5. "Gold Spot Prices," Goldhub (World Gold Council), accessed March 1, 2023, https://www.gold.org/goldhub/data/gold-prices.

Contact Information

Andrew Wommack Ministries, Inc.

PO Box 3333
Colorado Springs, CO 80934-3333
info@awmi.net
awmi.net

Helpline: 719-635-1111 (available 24/7)

Charis Bible College

info@charisbiblecollege.org
844-360-9577
CharisBibleCollege.org

For a complete list of all of our offices,
visit **awmi.net/contact-us**.

Connect with us on social media.